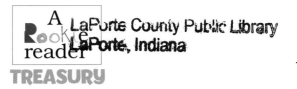

A
Rookie
reader
TREASURY

Family Photo

and Other
Family Stories

Children's Press®
An Imprint of Scholastic Inc.
New York • Toronto • London • Auckland • Sydney
Mexico City • New Delhi • Hong Kong
Danbury, Connecticut

Dear Rookie Reader,

Who are the people in
your family?
What do you do for fun?
Read about kids a lot like you.
They have fun with their
families, too!

Have fun and keep reading!

Don't forget to check out the fun
activities on pages 108–111!

Contents

Going to Grandma's Farm

By Betsy Franco

Illustrated by Claudia Rueda

We're going to our grandma's farm.

We ride in a cab.

We ride in a plane.

We ride on a boat.

We ride on a train.

We see Grandma!

We ride in her jeep.

Watch out for the sheep!

Beep! Beep! Beep!

Now we're all at
Grandma's farm.

We ride the horses from the barn!

Splat!

By Mary Margaret Pérez-Mercado
Illustrated by Richard L. Torrey

I helped my Dad.
We baked a cake.

I think it was
a big mistake.

The frosting fell.
It hit the floor.

It hit the wall.

It hit the door.

It hit the dog.

It hit the cat.

It hit my Dad
with one big . . .

SpL

It hit my Mom.

It hit my snake.

But it NEVER EVER
hit the cake!

Baby in the House

By David F. Marx
Illustrated by Cynthia Fisher

A baby is in the house,
and Eve is not happy.

The baby grabs too much.

The baby smells too much.

The baby costs too much.

The baby cries too much.

A baby is in the house,
and Eve is looking closer.

The baby laughs a lot.

The baby smells sweet.

The baby looks cute
in his new snowsuit.

A baby is in the house,
and Eve is playing with him.

The baby has great toys.

The baby reads Eve's books.

The baby pats Eve's face.

The baby holds on tight,

but Eve loves the baby.

A baby is in the house,
and Eve is happy.

Family Photo

By Dana Meachen Rau

Illustrated by Mike Gordon

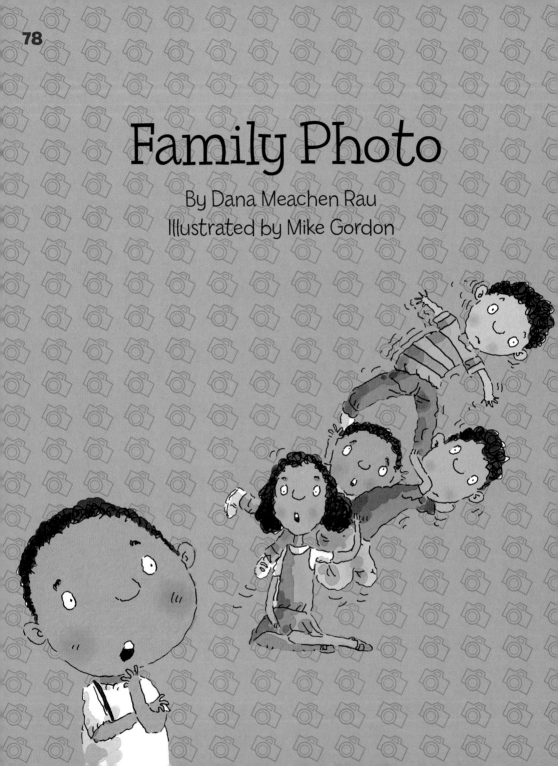

Grandpa, stand in the grass.

Grandma, sit on this chair.

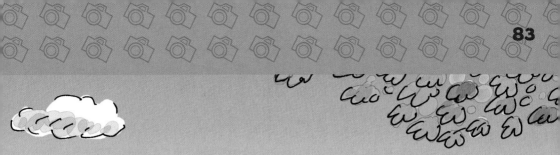

Uncle Joe, stand by the table.

Aunt Sue can stand over there.

Mom can sit beside
Grandpa.

Brother can sit on her lap.

Dad can stand with the baby. Someone wake up Spot from his nap.

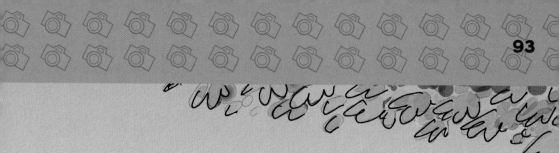

Big sister, stand on the left.
Little sister, stand on the right.

Hurry, everyone! Please stay still.
We can't do this all night!

Cousins, crowd close together.
I still can't see you all!

Tom, get onto Bob's shoulders.
Be careful not to fall!

Jack, stand behind Bob. We don't have a moment to spare!

Sally, come on over!
Can you kneel over
there?

I think I can see Cousin Fred
if he hangs upside down
from that tree.

Now everyone take out your cameras and take a picture of me!

Match the words and pictures.

Boat

Plane

Cab

The frosting never hit the _____.

dog   mom   cake   door

Happy or Unhappy?

Retell the story.

What made Eve unhappy?
What made her happy?

Lots of words rhyme with **all**.

How many can you name?

Hint: there is a clue in this picture.

Library of Congress Cataloging-in-Publication Data

Family photo and other family stories.
   p. cm. -- (A Rookie reader treasury)
   Contents: Going to Grandma's Farm / by Betsy Franco; illustrated by Claudia Rueda
                 Splat! / by Mary Margaret Pérez-Mercado; illustrated by Richard L. Torrey
                 Baby in the House / by David F. Marx; illustrated by Cynthia Fisher
                 Family Photo / by Dana Meachen Rau; illustrated by Mike Gordon

   ISBN-13: 978-0-531-21725-2
   ISBN-10: 0-531-21725-6

 1. Children's stories, American. [1. Short stories.]
 I. Title. II. Series.

PZ5.F2143 2008
[E]--dc22   2008008295

1 2 3 4 5 6 7 8 9 10 R 18 17 16 15 14 13 12 11 10 09